Seven Principles of Educational Success

Workbook

Seven Principles of Educational Success

Workbook

Dr. Juniace Sénécharles Etienne

Cataloging-in-Publication data for this book is available from the Library of Congress
ISBN:9781732592001

Cover and Graphics Design by: Carmen Luz Soler

This is a work of educational nonfiction. Personal events are portrayed to the best of the authors' memory. Some minor details may have been altered or changed. The information contained in this book is for informational purposes only.

Table of Contents

INTRODUCTION

The Purpose of this Workbook

You are discovering yourself, your personal purpose, and the purpose of your education. We are grateful to share this journey with you!

After having read the *Seven Principles for Educational Success*, we encourage you to make good use of the accompanying workbook and answer the questions in place for each chapter. These questions are tools to help you better assimilate the information.

This workbook will allow you to anchor your newly acquired knowledge by answering multiple-choice, fill-in-the-blank, and critical thinking questions, and completing a series of group activities. Most importantly, you will create a plan that will reflect your understanding of the concepts referenced in the book, such as your learning style, your college choices, your leading role in your sphere of influence, and your way of challenging yourself so that you can become your best self.

This workbook will help you apply to your own education the seven principles that we explored together, so that you can fulfill your personal purpose and carry out the purpose of your education.

Progress Map

On this page, you will find a progress map that can be used to keep track of your work as you make progress through the workbook and focus on each of the seven principles. The map also comes in handy when you want to add some comments about each of the concepts.

	Learning Goal	✓	Comments
# 1	To discover my purpose		
# 2	To understand my kind of intelligence and learning style		
# 3	To establish a personal academic plan		
# 4	To establish personal academics goals		
# 5	To discover my own leadership essence		
# 6	To use My College Option as a tool to accomplish my plan		
# 7	To understand how I can challenge myself		

PRINCIPLE

#1

Self-Discovery

The Essential Question

What can we do to understand the Self-discovery process?

Objective

After reading this text, you will be able to understand the importance of the Self-discovery process, and the various ways to discover oneself.

Presentation of the Course

Topics of Discussion and Reflection

1. How can you explain the complexity of the Self-discovery process?
2. What are the results when the discovery of self has not been achieved?

Exercises:

1. Explain why Self-discovery is not an easy task.
2. What are the guidelines to be followed during the process of Self-discovery?
3. Why is it important to have an educational purpose?
4. What is the purpose of your education?
5. How can you avoid an educational catastrophe?
6. Discuss three of the twelve steps in determining your academic purpose.

Assessment

Homework:

1. Have you discovered something new about yourself? Did you learn a bit more about an aspect of yourself that you were already aware of – maybe something that others had already mentioned?
2. What changes are you going to put in place to apply this new knowledge?
3. How do you intend to share this statement with other people?
4. What problems does Self-discovery solve?
5. Should everyone go through the process of Self-discovery? Explain your answer.
6. In your opinion, what are two good reasons for someone to go through the process of

Self-discovery?

7. What might you need to better understand the Self-discovery process?

Presentation:

Do you believe that you have the potential to be successful? You can either write or draw your answer. Use as many details as possible to demonstrate your understanding of the question.

Group Activity:

Work with a small group to go over each other's answers to the Self-discovery survey questions. What are the similarities? What are the differences? Use a Venn Diagram or another type of chart to help you illustrate your answers.

PRINCIPLE

#2

This is how I Learn

The Essential Questions

1. Can everyone learn?
2. What is the difference between intelligence and successful intelligence?

Objective

After reading this text, you will be able to understand the importance of targeting multiple intelligences, and find out your own type of intelligence.

Presentation of the Course

Topic of Discussion and Reflection

1. Do you think that a lack of activities targeting Multiple Intelligence (MI) in the classrooms may affect a student's education? Why? Or why not?

Exercises:

1. Who is Howard Gardner?
2. What do we mean by Multiple Intelligences (MI)?
3. How many types of MI exist? How many of them can you identify? Why?
4. Discuss the three types of intelligence to which you are the least familiar.
5. Discuss the one intelligence that might apply to your learning style.
6. Why do you think it is important to understand the theory of multiple intelligences?

Assessment

Homework:

1. What is the key to knowing your strengths in order to improve your weaknesses?
2. Do you think people are born with multiple intelligences (MI)? Explain.
3. Do you agree with Gardner that people's intelligences establish the way they access and process information? Explain how apply to you this statement?
4. Do you agree that our individual backgrounds, abilities, challenges and skills make us learn differently?

Critical Thinking

1. Which feature of MI could help you enhance your education? Give an example. Write your answer on a separate sheet of paper.
2. How would you use the knowledge of MI to improve your education?

Group Activity:

Work with a small group to discuss what would be different if all students knew how they learn. One group member takes notes during the discussion. The remaining group members can write a short essay to explain how learning would be if all students knew and understood how they learn materials and concepts that are presented to them in class or outside of class. In the essay, explain which of the MI you can identify with, or which one is irrelevant to you.

PRINCIPLE

#3

Planning for Success

The Essential Questions

1. What are the benefits of planning?
2. Can success be accomplished without planning?
3. Can you take a trip without planning it? Why or why not?
4. Can we build a house without a blueprint? Why or why not?

Objectives

After reading this text, you will be able to understand the importance of planning.
You will be able to create an effective plan to achieve a specific goal.

Presentation of the Course

Topic of Discussion and Reflection

Is it possible that a good planning can affect your educational future positive or negatively?

Exercises:

Fill in the blank

1. Effective planning can _____ reach _____.
2. A _____ plan will help you to learn how to prioritize your time and how to stay _____ in order to achieve success.
3. A well-thought out plan will _____ you to define and _____ standards for your studies.

Assessment

Homework:

Fill in the blanks:

1. Proper planning is a crucial step to achieve your _____
2. Planning will help you stay _____ and take control of your _____ and
3. Your academic journey can be impacted by many _____ and

4. You need to take the _____ to write the necessary _____ to achieve your goal.

Critical Thinking

What procedure should you follow when writing your plan? Create a yearly plan to illustrate the steps and procedures that you will apply to accomplish your educational purpose.

Activity Option: Think of an educational goal that you have already set for yourself. If you don't have a goal in mind, take a few minutes to create a goal. Examples of goals include, but are not limited to: submitting college applications, joining a school club or an academic team, getting your driver's license, etc. Next, think of a timeline for accomplishing your goal. Now work backwards to design a plan that will ensure the success of that goal. What are some things that you will need to do within the next 2 weeks – or the next 30, 60, or even 90 days – to reach the point of completion? Use a calendar to draft your ideas, goals, expectations, and anticipated deadlines. Share this information with a parent, counselor, teacher, or close friend. Allow that person to be your accountability partner to ensure that you reach your goals and create sustainable plans for your life.

Group Activity

Work with a small group to write 3-5 questions about the planning process. Create a board with images to present the answers

PRINCIPLE

#4

Defining your Objectives

The Essential Questions

1. Why is it important to set goals or to have objectives?
2. What does it mean to have a final product?
3. Is it possible to be successful without having a goal?

Objective

After reading this text, you will be able to understand the importance of planning effectively.

Presentation of the Course

Topics of Discussion and Reflection

1. What is a goal?
2. Is it necessary to have a goal? Why? Why not?

Exercises:

Fill in the blank

1. Goal setting is the _____ to visualize the final product of a project in _____ steps.
2. When _____ your goals, you should be very _____ and straightforward.
3. If you want to know that you are on the right track for the Honor Roll or whichever goal you may have in mind, you have to be able to _____ your progress.
4. Your goal should be _____.
5. The key is: Your goal should have a _____ time and _____ time.
6. "If you want to be effective, you have to be _____ in your daily lives."
7. The best way to prioritize your_____is by having a set of goals.
8. Only a _____ things are necessary.

Assessment

Homework:

1. What is goal setting? (S.M.A.R.T.) How can you apply it in your life?
2. How is time management relevant to your plan?

Critical Thinking

Activity Option: Using one of the goals mentioned in the previous chapter, apply the S.M.A.R.T principles to your goal. Write your SMART plans in your journal or the workbook and refer to them daily for 21 days.

Group Activity

Work with a small group to list three goals and the steps to achieve each of these goals. Create a vision board to present that information.

PRINCIPLE

#5

Becoming a Leader

The Essential Questions

1. Can anyone in the whole world become a leader?
2. Is everyone in the world born to be a leader?
3. Does everyone have the necessary skills to become a leader?

Objectives

After reading this text, you will be able to define the concept of a leader, and to understand why the world has the elements necessary to become a leader.

Presentation of the Course

Topic of Discussion and Reflection

1. How can we become leaders?
2. Are people who occupy positions within the government the only leaders?
3. Why is it important that you discover your capacity for leadership?

Exercises:

Fill in the blank

1. We all have the _____ to lead within our spheres of I _____
2. If you know _____ you are, then you are on the right track to lead within those spheres because the abilities are in _____ await to be discovered.
3. The principle of leadership is _____ "self-serving" _____ "selfless service."
4. Being a leader is not about _____ others, but _____ them through influence.
5. You are a _____ and there is a spirit of _____ waiting to be unleashed within you.

Assessment

Homework:

1. How does Webster define a *leader*? Give examples of a leader.
2. Do you believe you have what it takes to be a leader? Why or why not?
3. Discuss one of the students' examples and how it might relate to you.

Critical Thinking

What can a leadership seminar teach you? How do leaders continually build their capacity to lead? What is the difference between a leader and a follower?

Group Activity

Work with a small group to write at least three to five characteristics a person should know about a leader. Then share your list with another group. Edit your list to include items listed by the other group.

Alternative activity option: Work within a small group. Create a t-chart. Label one side "A Great Leader Is…" and the other "A Great Leader Is Not…" Then work with your group to generate a list of common characteristics of effective and ineffective leadership. It is important to develop a balanced concept of what true/good leadership should reflect.

PRINCIPLE

#6

My College Option

The Essential Question

What are the benefits of having a college profile?

Objective

After reading this text, you will be able to understand how to create a college profile to increase your chance of getting accepted to the college of your choice.

Topics of Discussion and Reflection

1. What is the purpose of a college profile?
2. What measures have the universities decided to take with students who are not able to graduate on time? Why?
3. Why do many first-year students drop out of college?
4. What do you think about adopting the "My College Option" approach in your educational system?
5. Do you think that your educational system could benefit from a program like that? Whether you answer yes or no, please explain.

Presentation of the Course

Exercises:

Fill in the blanks

1. If your purpose is not supported with the right _____ there is no guarantee you can avoid _____
2. The _____ challenge in your academic journey is acknowledging the significant value of prioritizing your _____

Assessment

Homework:

1. What is the purpose of the College Options questionnaire?
2. What percentage of students generally change their major? How is this number relevant to you?

Critical Thinking

A friend tells you about My College Option. What type of information can you find about college?

Group Activity

Work with a group to create a flyer about My College Option. Include as much information as possible to illustrate the benefits of the program.

Pretend you are a high school guidance counselor who wants to create awareness about My College Option. Create a flyer that highlights the important aspects of the program. Be sure to include details, illustrations, and other important information that will demonstrate the benefits of the program.

PRINCIPLE

#7

Take the Challenge: Self-Empowerment

The Essential Questions

1. What are some challenges that can impact your generation? The next generation?
2. Why is it important to understand that there is a process in everything you will do?

Objective

After reading this text, you will be able to understand the concept of self-empowerment

You will be able to understand the objectives of a challenge and how to effectively achieve success.

Presentation of the Course

Topics of Discussion and Reflection

1. Why is it important to understand your challenges? What are some approaches that you need to apply in order to achieve success?
2. Have you ever applied a particular process to obtain a specific result? Explain.
3. The authors state that a process is a necessary tool for understanding Self-discovery. How can you elaborate on that statement?

Exercises:

1. How can you challenge yourself?
2. Why is it important to allow yourself to be challenged?
3. How would you change the world?

Assessment

Homework:

Fill in the blank

1. Challenging yourself will _____ you from being average to _____.
2. Your _____ must go through a _____ in order to become valuable.
3. Process is how you will _____ yourself and accept the tasks required to become successful.

Critical Thinking

What are the purposes of a challenge?

Embedded in every challenge is the opportunity for growth. Reflect on a moment where you experienced an important challenge. Examples can include, but are not limited to, learning a new instrument, moving to a new school, joining a sports team, applying for college. Now, reflect on how that challenge prompted a level of growth and maturity within you. How were you able to move from the initial challenge, to growth and/or success? Journal about your experience.

Group Work

Work with a group to discuss the advice you would give someone who may be having a difficult time identifying his/her purpose. Be sure to include information about Self-discovery, multiple intelligences, planning, and other applicable concepts if necessary.

Create a PowerPoint or use another media to present that information.

The Passion Ball

After having read the *Seven Principles workbook* and completed the activities designed to improve your understanding, you are now ready to apply your newly acquired knowledge about these principles, along with your creative skills. You will create a 12-sided "Passion Ball" that will incorporate each one of the elements listed below.

It's important to remember that all writing and decorating should be done on each pentagon **before you cut and fold the sides**. You may add decorations or drawings to any unused space on the paper.

The sides are as follows:

Side 1- Passion: Write down your name, your Passion, your Vision and your Sphere of influence, and some sort of illustration representing your Passion.

Side 2 - Who are you?: Write your bio or you can draw pictures. Provide your name and list some interesting facts about yourself. Why did you choose this passion? (3-5 sentences).

Side 3 - Your Character (How you learn): Describe your character with words or pictures. Include both physical and personality traits. Include one quote to describe your character. (3-5 sentences).

Side 4 - Spheres of Influence: Draw a picture describing where you would like to put your passion into play.

Side 5 - Reasons: Identify the reasons why you want to carry out this passion, this vision. Is it for you, your family, your community, or the world? You can write or use pictures (3-5 sentences).

Side 6 - Tell us what you know: Opinion: Tell us what people say about your passion. You can also use pictures or images. Who told you about it? (2-3 sentences).

Sides 7 & 8 - Requirements: Split the section about your passion in half and write short-term and long-term goals to carry it out. **On Side 7,** write the short-term goals (Present, NOW). **On Side 8,** write the long-term goals (within one or two years, or more). All the goals should be S.M.A.R.T. goals (3-5 sentences on each pentagon).

Side 9 - College/University: Draw a picture of the college/university/vocational school you would like to attend in order to carry out your passion.

Side 10 - Alternate Side: Write 3-5 sentences or use images (pictures) that will allow you to visualize yourself graduating from college/university to pursue your passion.

Side 11- Quote (Advice): Include an important quote or advice you have received about your passion. Why is this advice so important to you? Use your creativity to add color and images to this circle to help showcase the quote and its importance as it relates to your passion.

Side 12 - Relate: Write 3-5 sentences or use images (pictures) explaining how you feel connected to this passion. How can this passion change your life, or the lives of other people?

When all sides and decorations are complete:

- Carefully cut out the 12 pentagons.
- Fold the crescents on the lines around the pentagon so that the folds are standing up or facing up.
- Align the crescent of one pentagon to the crescent of another and staple them together (glued pentagons might become unglued). Each side will be stapled to a different side all the way around to create a ball.
- Be sure that all edges are facing up and are framing your pictures or sentences.

REMEMBER

- Be neat!
- The ball should be colorful and visually appealing, but the most important aspect is what is written or drawn on the sides.
- Use your creativity, your gift, and your talents. Be bold and be YOU!
- Remember, you are putting your passion on display!

Label the Side

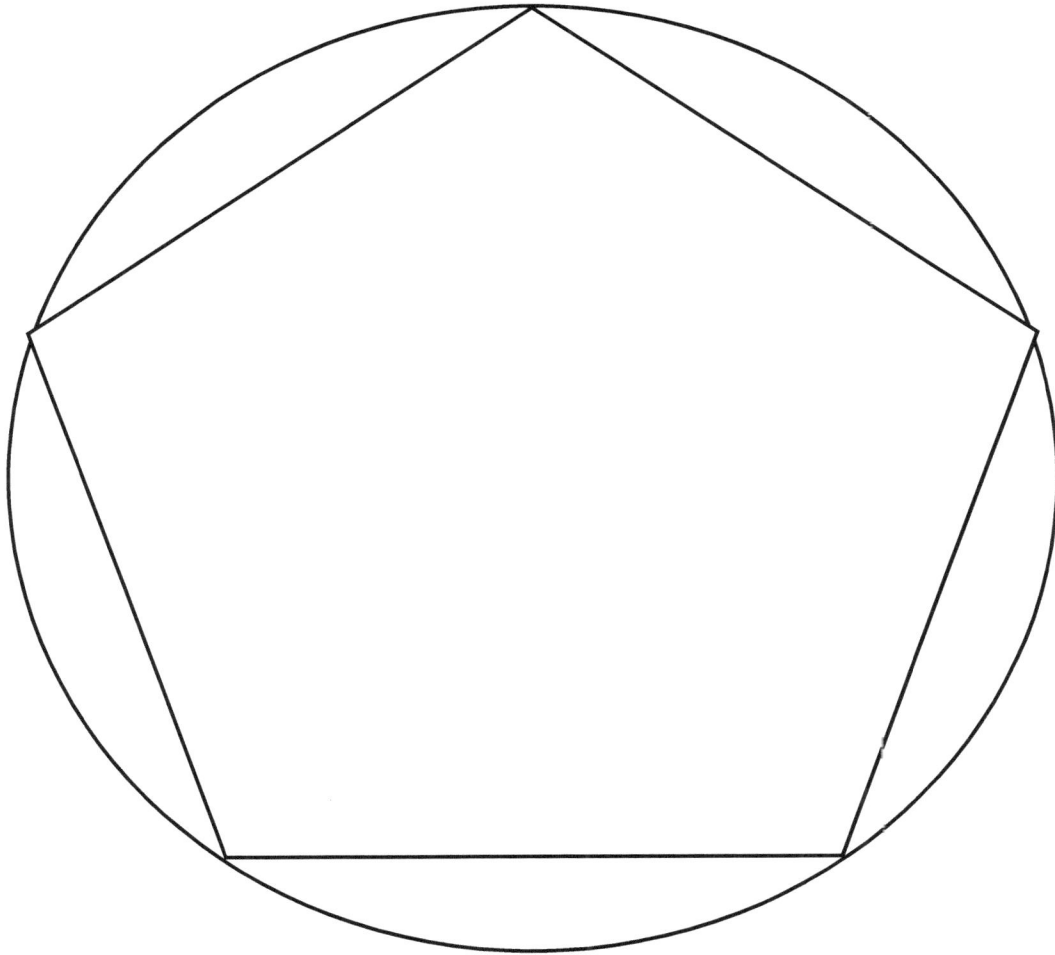

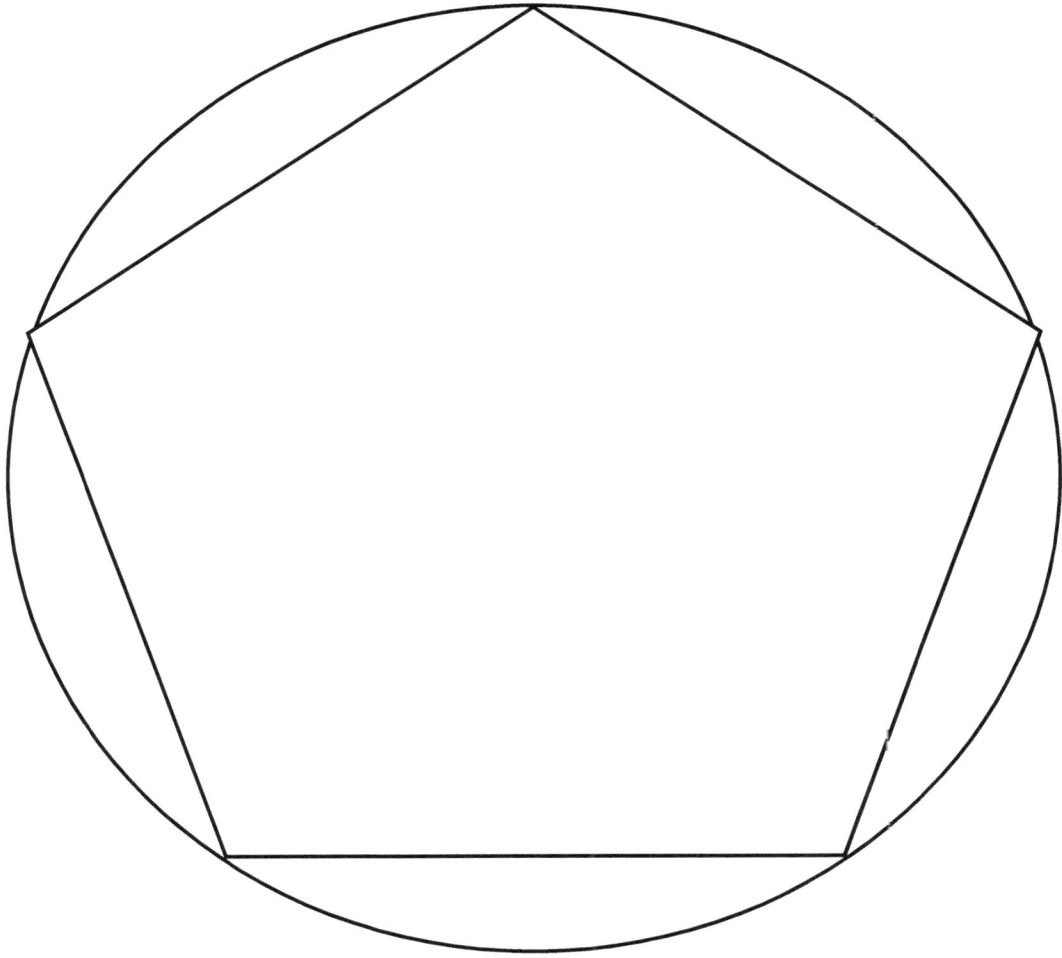

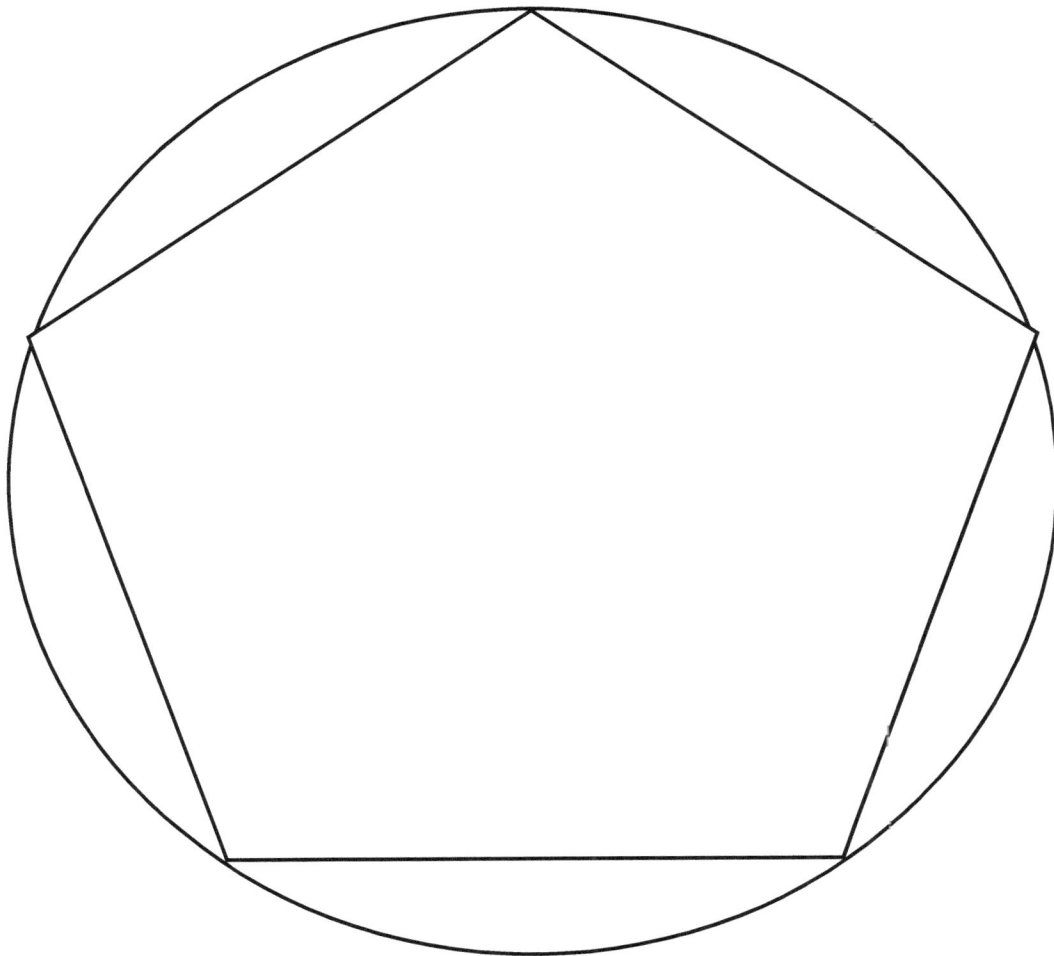

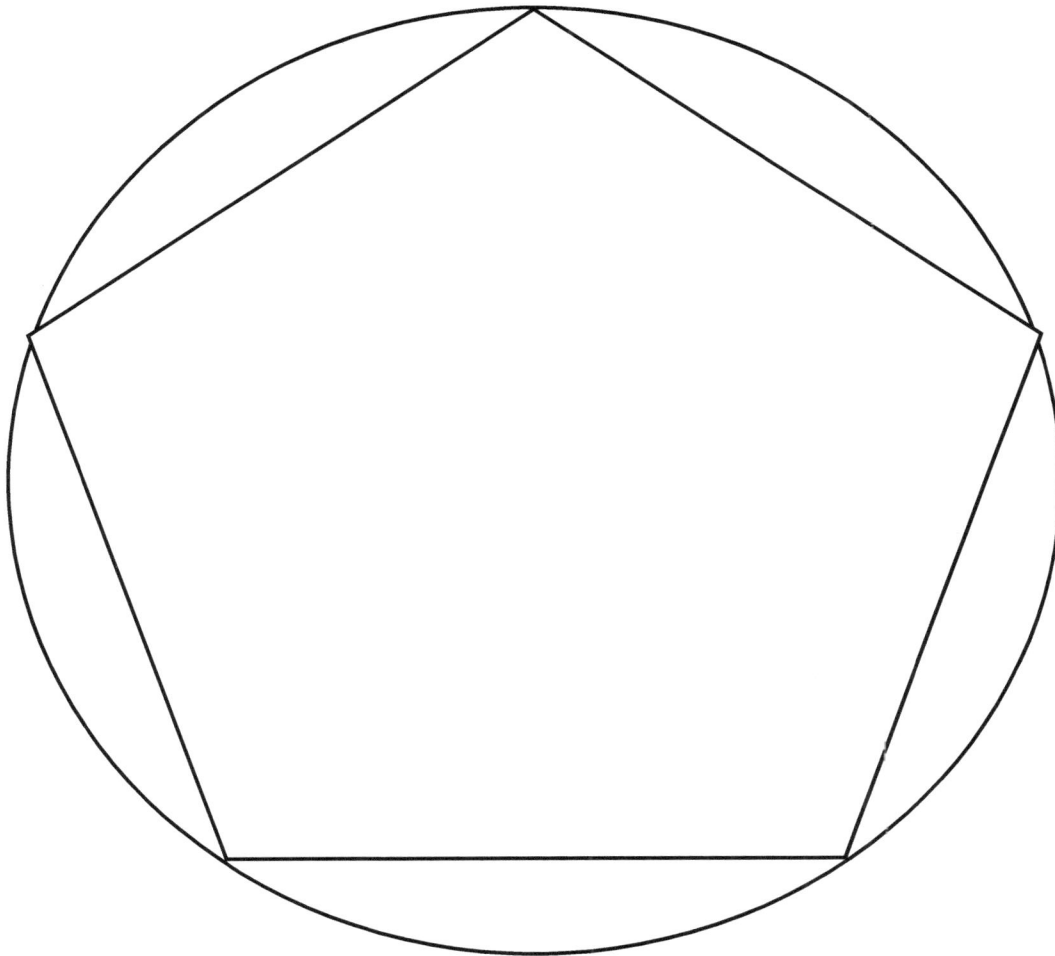

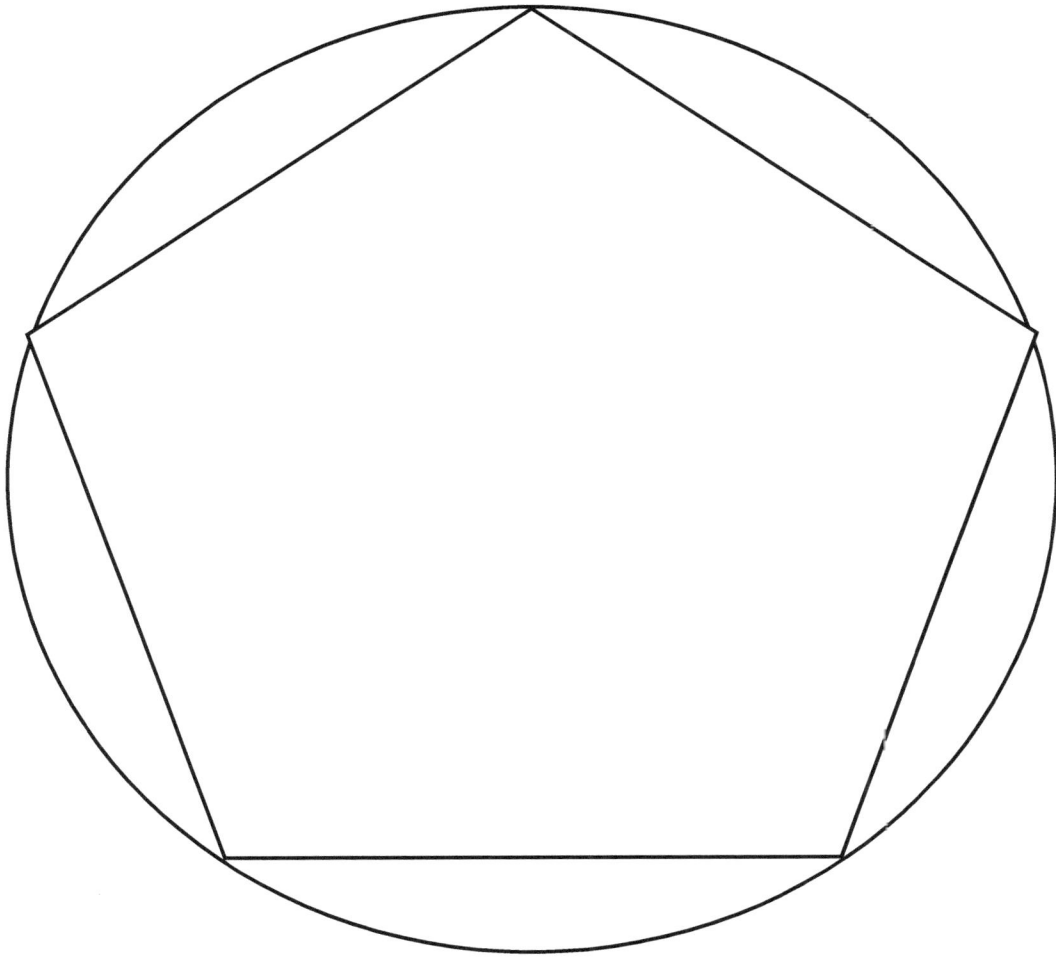

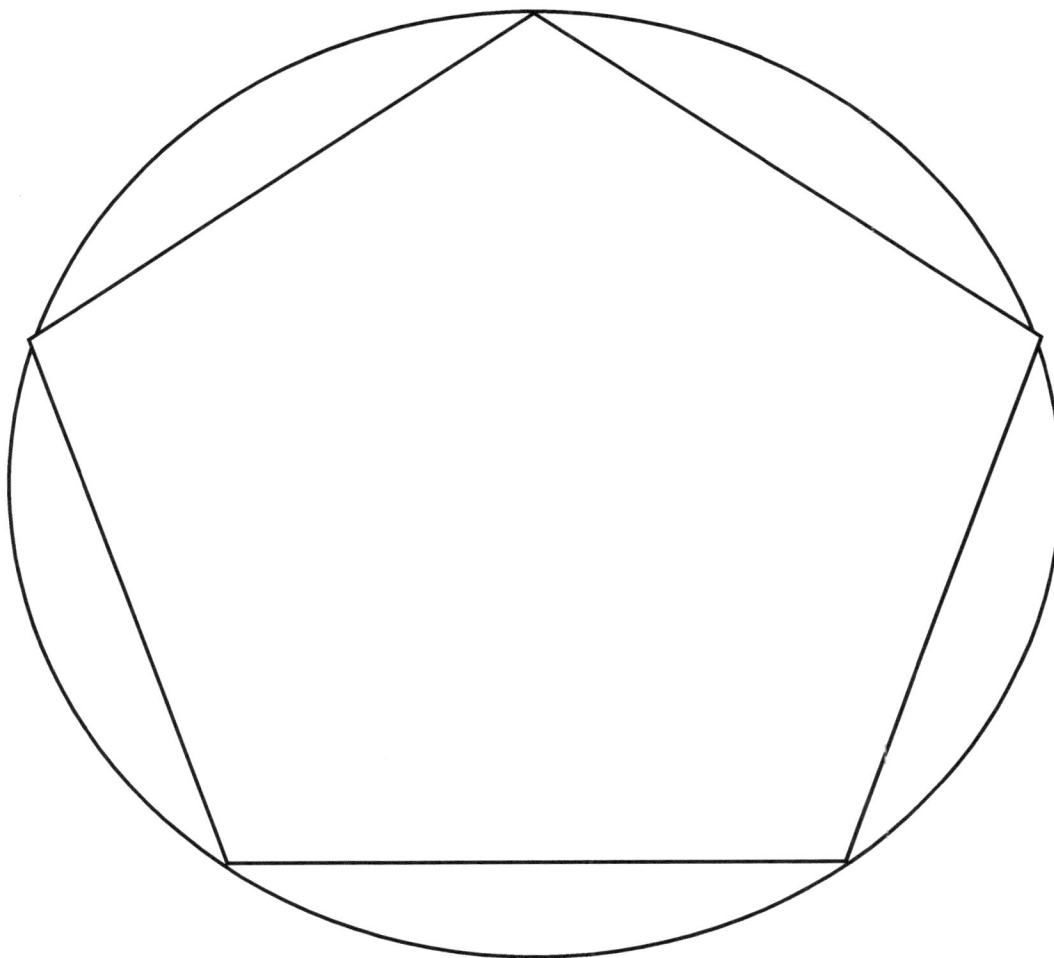

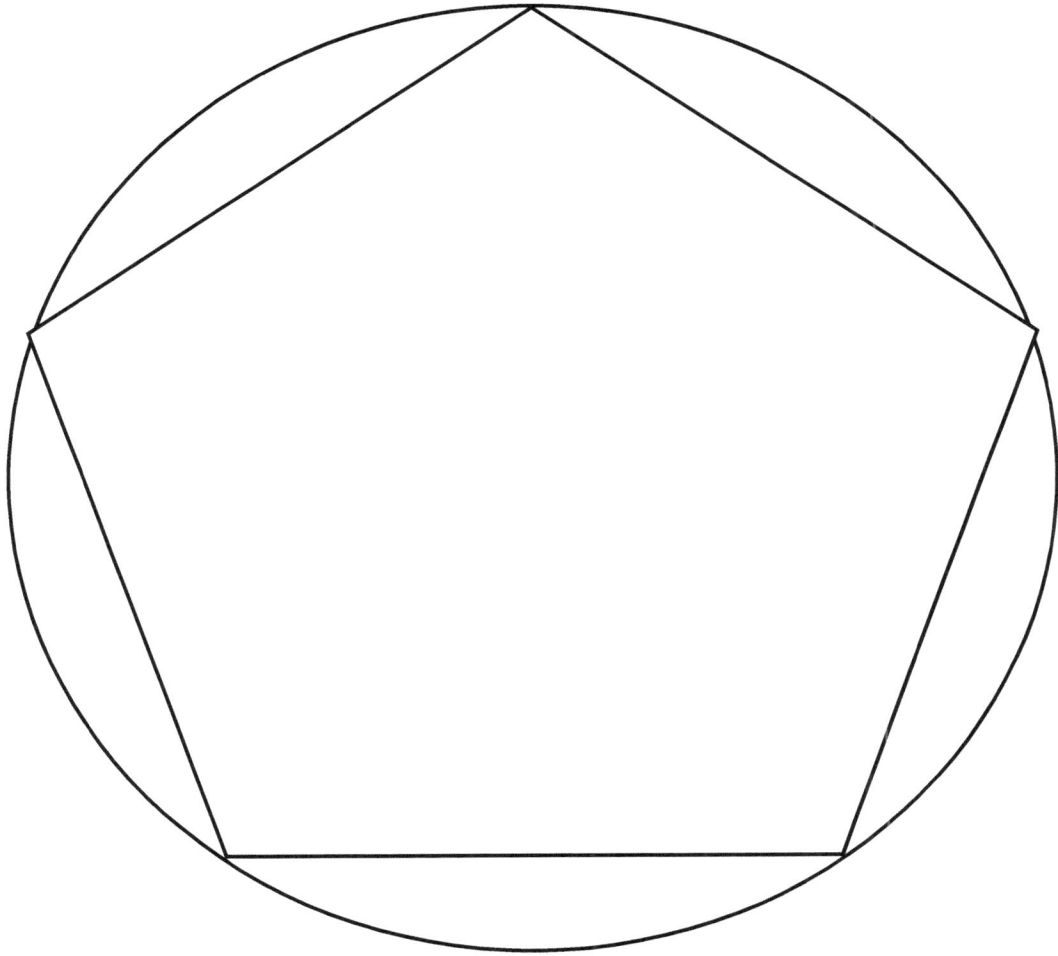

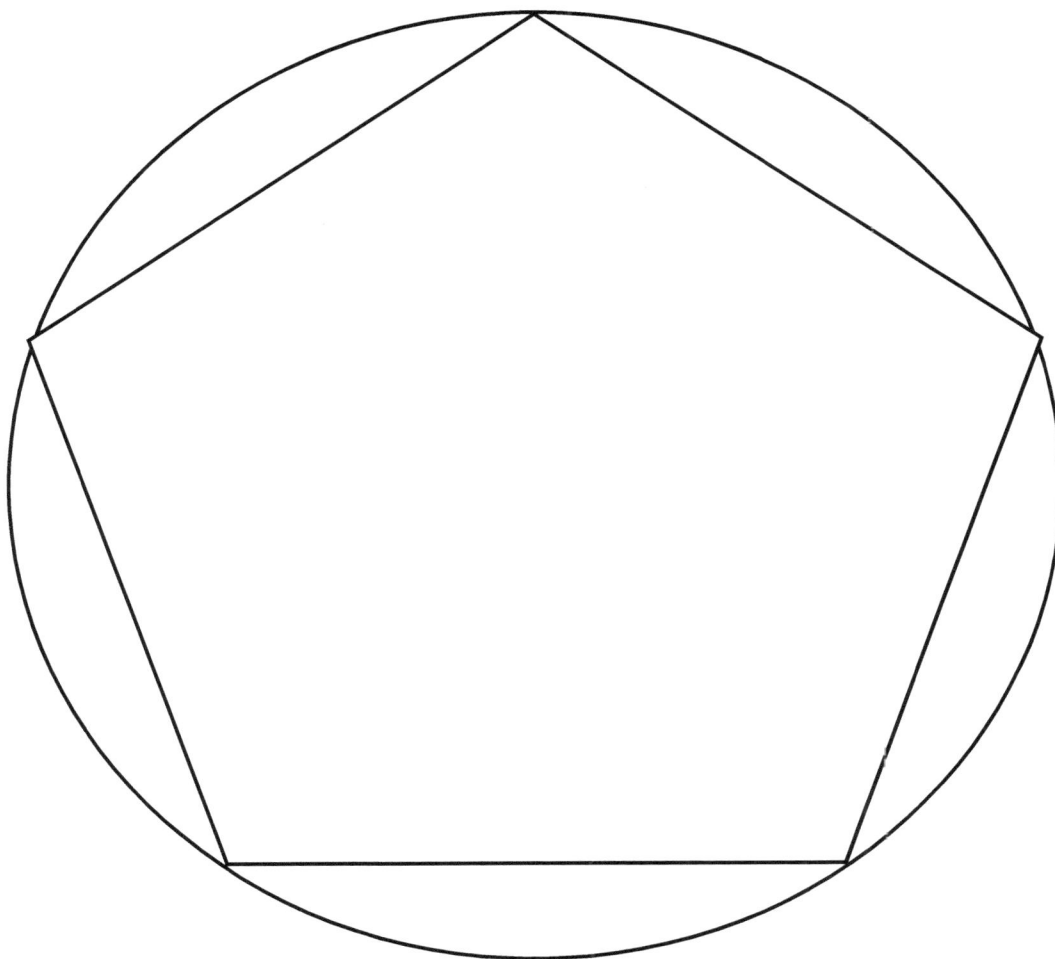

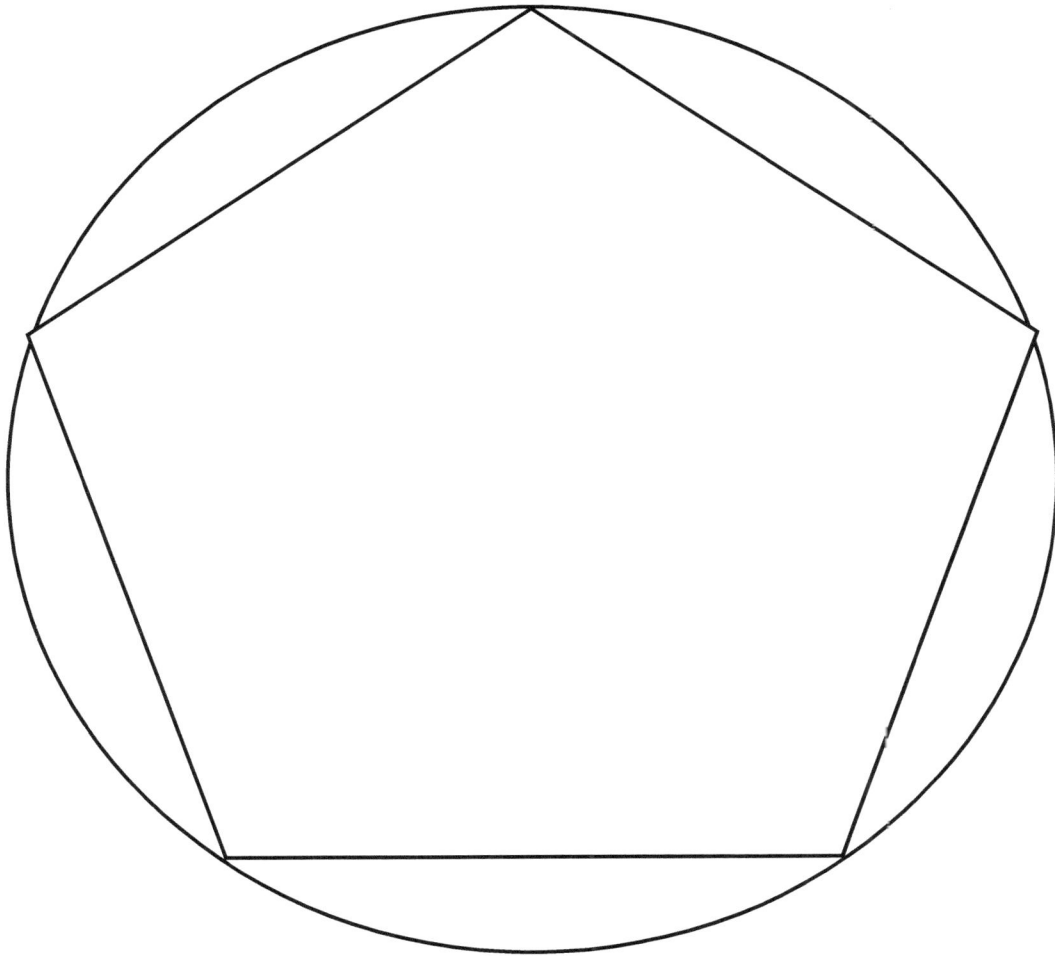

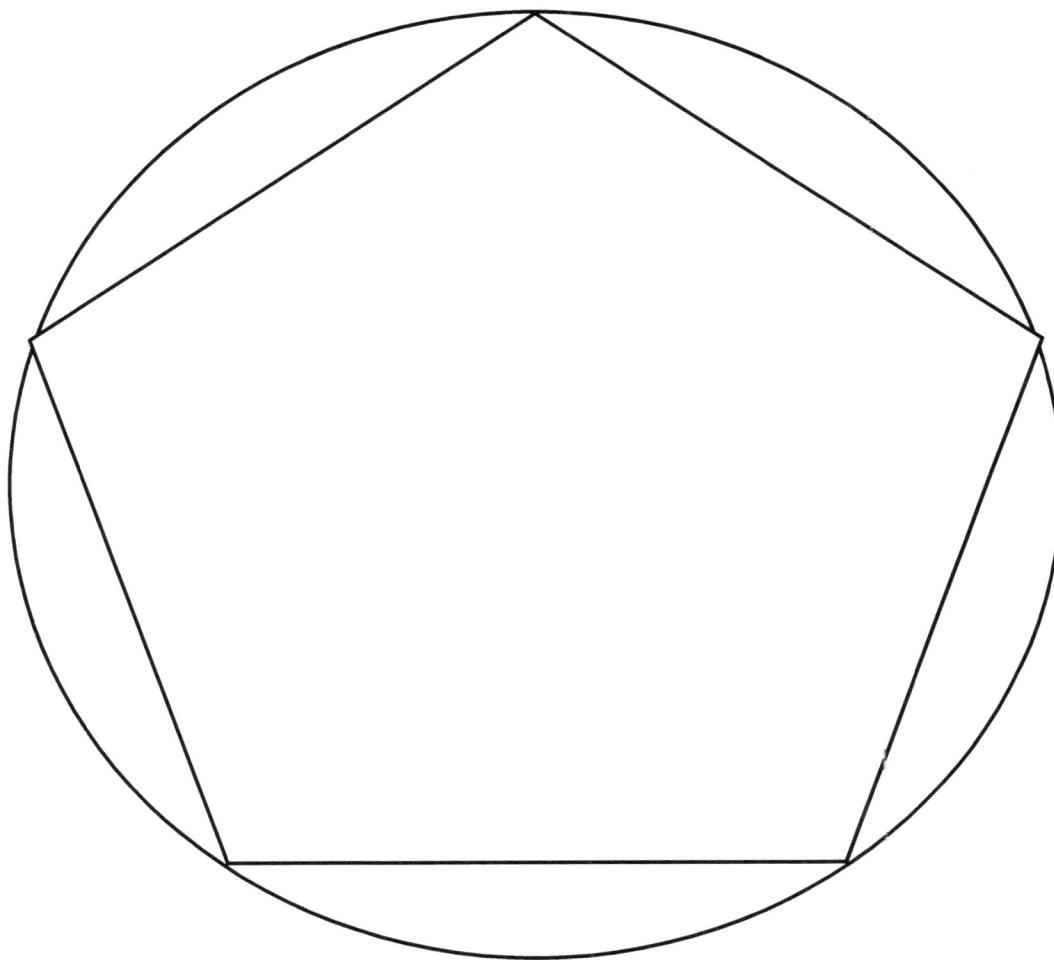

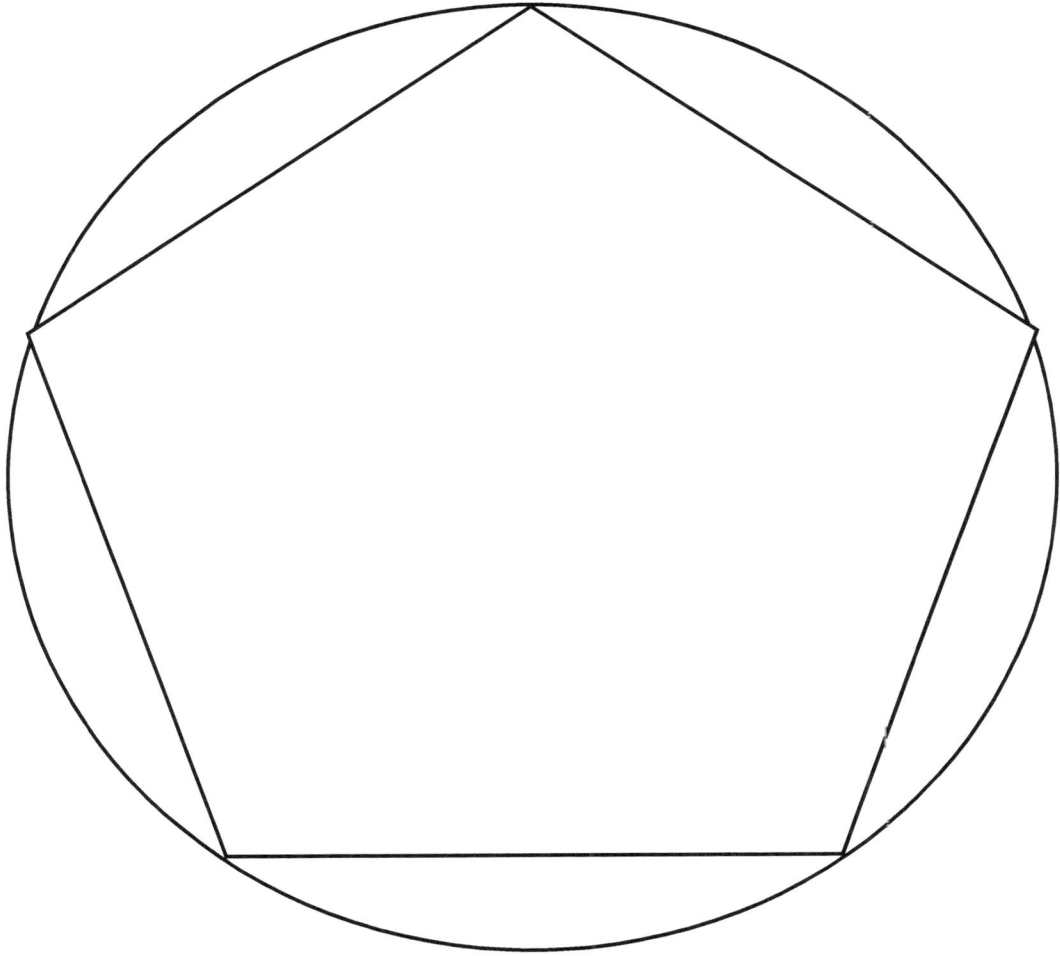

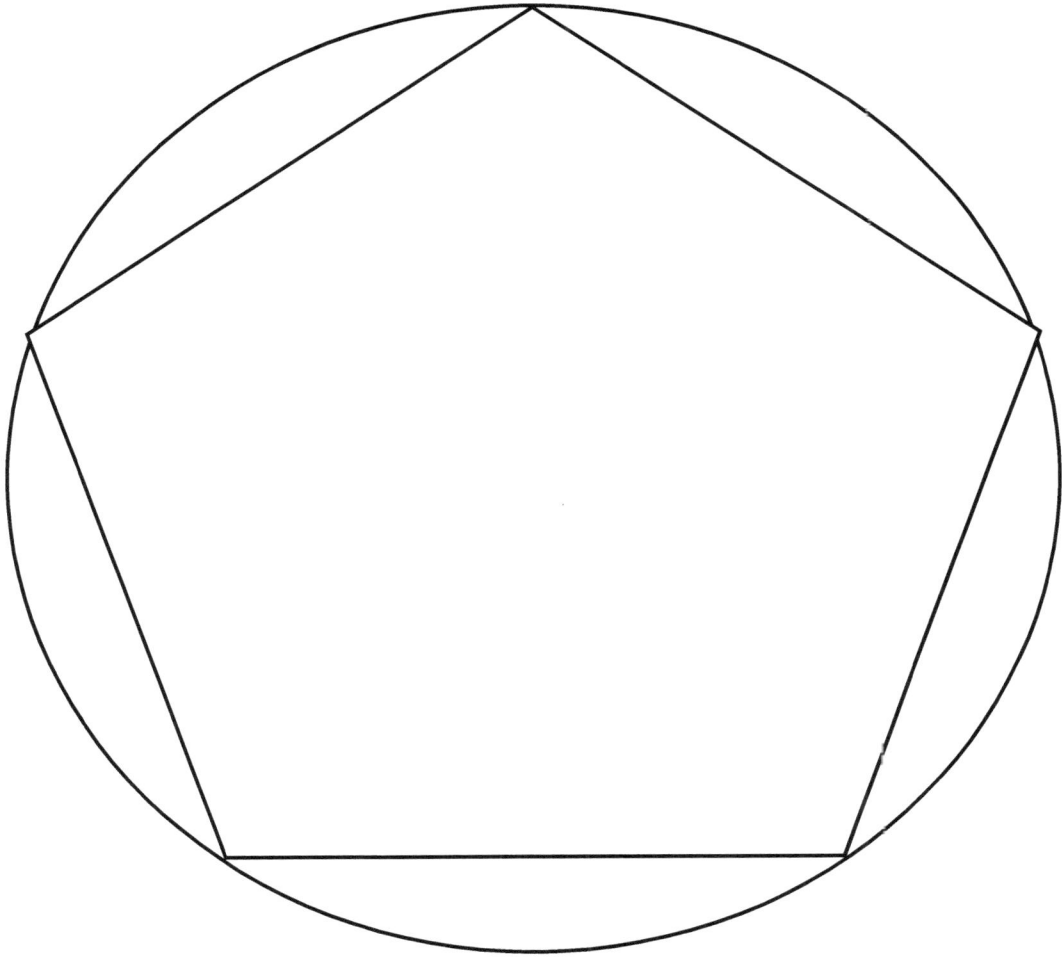

My Way Out – Passion Pathway

My name is: _____ I am ____ years old

I am passionate about _____ .

I have many gifts and talents. I am particularly good at _____

_____ .

I really enjoy _____ .

My Support system consists of:

- Family Members
  - a.
  - b.
- Friends
  - a.
  - b.

- Teachers/Counselors
  - a.
  - b.
- Professionals/Community Members
  - a.
  - b.

My Way Out in 10 Steps

1. Diploma/Credential Status Year Earned _____

   - ☐ High School Diploma
   - ☐ General Education
       Diploma (GED)

   - ☐ Join the Workforce
       Without a Diploma
   - ☐ Foreign Credentials
       Earned & Evaluated

2. Post-Secondary Pathway

   - ☐ College/University
   - ☐ Vocational or Trade School
   - ☐ Military- Branch _____

   - ☐ Industry Apprenticeship
   - ☐ Professional Certifications
   - ☐ Entrepreneur

3. Study Major/Domain _____ & Entry Requirements

   - ☐ GPA Minimum Score _____
   - ☐ ACT Score _____
   - ☐ SAT Score _____

   - ☐ TABE Score _____
   - ☐ Other Test Score _____
   - ☐ No Testing Requirements

4. Projected Job Growth Rate/Outlook (https://www.bls.gov) _____

5. Time Investment

    ☐ 3-9 month   ☐ 12 months   ☐ 12-18 months
    ☐ 2 years   ☐ 3-5 years   ☐ 6-10 years

6. Location & Housing Cost $_____ total.

    ☐ In-state
       o   Local- Live at Home
       o   Local- Private Housing Arrangements
       o   Relocate to new city- Private Housing Arrangements
    ☐ Out-of-state- Private Housing Arrangements
    ☐ International- Private Housing Arrangements

7. Tuition/Start-Up Cost $_____ total for all Time Invested

8. Payment Plan (Funding Sources)

    ☐   Grants/Academic Scholarships   ☐ Pre-Paid College/University Fund
    ☐   Athletic Scholarships   ☐ Pay as I go (Work & Study)
    ☐   Partial/Full Funded by Parents   ☐ Institutional Loans (Banks/Government)
    ☐   Paid Apprenticeship/Internship   ☐ Personal Loans (Friends/Family)

9. Career Outcomes

    ▪ Anticipated Completion Year_____
    ▪ Professional Title _____
    ▪ Earning Potential $ _____ (Entry Level)

10. Service with a Purpose

    ▪   Whom will you serve? I will serve _____

    How will you serve them? I will serve them by_____

*Gifts & Talents

* Support System

1. Diploma/Credential Status YEAR-

2. Post-Secondary Pathway

3. Study Major/ Domain & Requirements

4. Projected Job Growth/Outlook

5. Time Investment

6. Location & Housing Cost

7. Total Tuition/ Start-up Cost

8. Payment Plan

9. Career Outcomes

10. Service with a Purpose

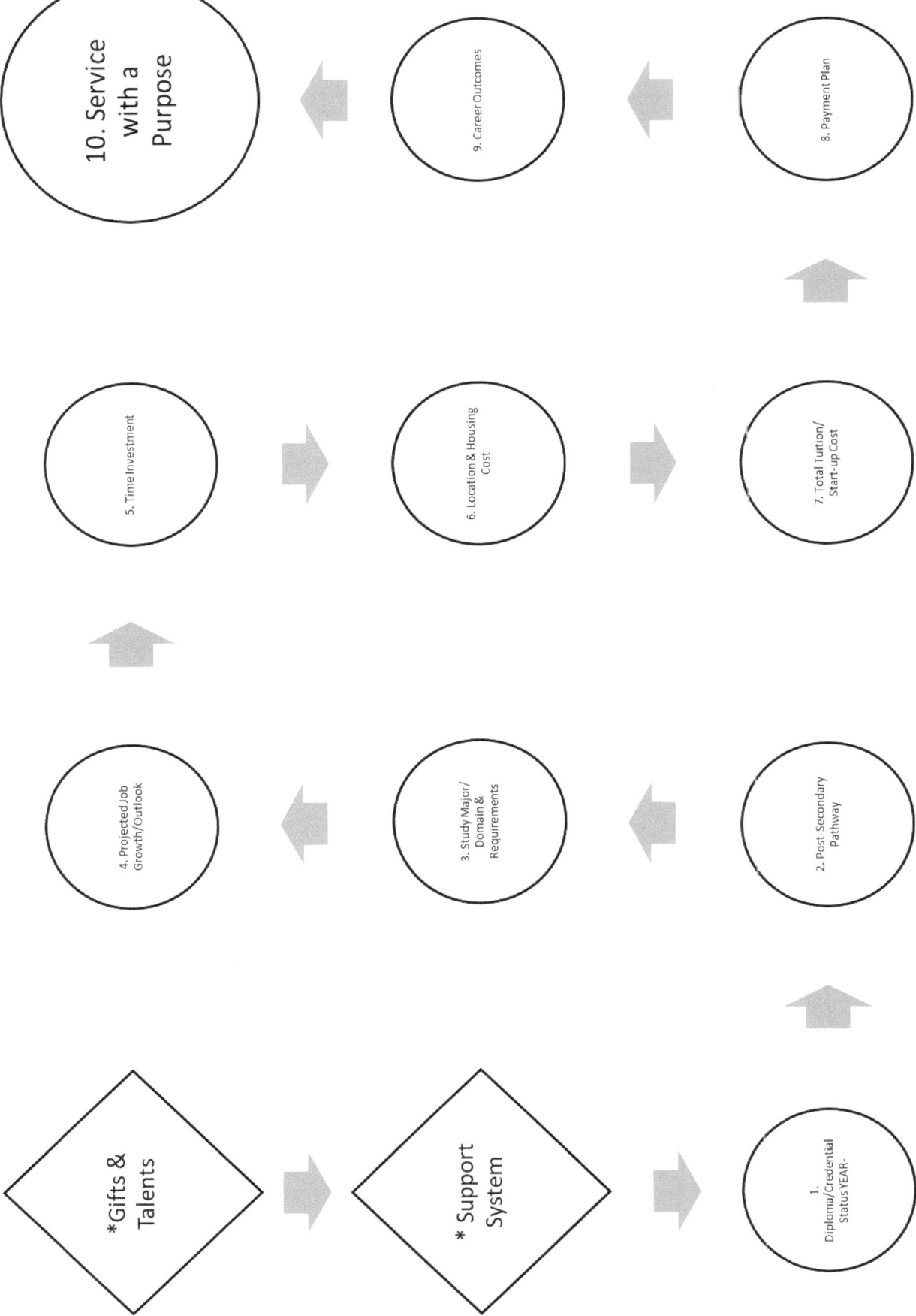

Enter →

Exit →

*Gifts & Talents

* Support System

1. Diploma/Credential Status YEAR

2. Post-Secondary Pathway

3. Study Major/Domain & Requirements

4. Projected Job Growth/Outlook

5. Time Investment

6. Location & Housing Cost

7. Total Tuition / Start-up Cost

8. Payment Plan

9. Career Outcomes

10. Service with a Purpose

About the Authors

Dr. Juniace Sénécharles Etienne is a French teacher with the Collier Public Schools in Naples, Florida. Dr. Etienne works with children at all academic skill levels, including those with special needs and those who are academically gifted. In addition to teaching, Dr. Etienne is a published writer whose work includes *Three Steps to Guide Your Children's Educational Future*. She is an international speaker and educational consultant. Recent lecture topics include Goal Setting, Prioritizing for a Successful High School Experience, Preparing for a Successful Parent/Teacher Conference, Preparing our 21st Century Student for Academic Success, and Planning for Life after High School. Dr. Etienne was the lead campaign coordinator in the United States for Haiti's 2015-2016 presidential elections.

Dr. Etienne graduated Summa Cum Laude from Barry University. She earned a master's degree in Reading, from Nova Southern University and a doctoral degree in Teacher Leadership, from Walden University. Further, she is pursuing a Master of Arts in Romance Languages at University of New Orleans (UNO). She is married to Romel Etienne and is the mother of four wonderful daughters: Joyce, Jessica, Samantha, and Sheena.

A native of Miragôane, Haiti, Dr. Etienne migrated to the United States at the age of 16 and knows firsthand that education can expand one's opportunities to succeed. Her passion is to empower her students and stimulate their intellectual curiosity. One of her goals is to inform world leaders about the importance of accessible education and its necessity in creating a stronger future for our children.

Paulina Soto Vasquez is a Chilean psychologist and university teacher. She is also the mother of two beautiful children, Trinidad Avila and Federico Avila. She lives in Chile with her husband Felipe.

She worked as a psychologist in public health for six years. Although she experienced joy helping other people, something was missing: she knew she could contribute significantly more to society. It was not until she discovered that she was a gifted educator that she decided to share her vision with others in the field.

Pursuing a master's degree in Educational Psychology, Ms. Vasquez introduces integral development principles in academic environments, incorporating these principles into the classes she designs and in her interactions with students. She is developing psych educational programs and audiovisual materials to help others release their full potential.

This is her first book, and it was a beautiful collaborative work with Dr. Sénécharles.

Other Works by Dr. Etienne

A Grounded Theory Approach to Use of Differentiate Instruction to Improve Students' Outcomes in Mathematics. Walden University: scholar works, 2011.

Three Steps to Guide Your Children Educational Future. Regenz Book, 2014.

Three Steps to Guide Your Children's Educational Future. 2nd edition. Juniace Shaping Young Minds LLC, 2017

Triumphing Over Hell on Earth. Maverick Press, 2015.

References

"Attribution-ShareAlike 3.0 Unported (CC BY-SA 3.0)" *Creative Commons.*
http://creativecommons.org/licenses/by-sa/3.0/)

"Biafra". *English @ CC.* https://ncowie.wordpress.com/2010/07/26/biafra/

Bible Gateway. https://www.biblegateway.com/

Etienne, Juniace. Three Steps to Guide Your Children Educational Future. *Juniace Shaping Young Minds*, LLC, 2015.

Etienne, J, & Philippi, D. *My Way Out, 2018.*

Financing the Future. http://financingthefuture.org

Http://en.wikipedia.org/wiki/Day_of_Seven_Billion/

"Hunger Games Images" https://ncowie.wordpress.com/page/35/

Kragh, Trista Sue. "How to Write your Personal Vision." *Kingdom Connection Newsletter.* 2010. www.TristaSue.com

Kragh, Trista Sue. *Figure it Out.* Maverick Press, 2015.

Munroe, M. *The principles and power of vision: keys to achieving personal and corporate destiny.* New Kensington, PA: Whitaker House, 2003.

Munroe, M. Understand your potential. *Discovering the Hidden you,* Destiny Image Publishers, Inc., 2003.

Penn State. "Earth in the Future". *E.education.* https://www.e-education.psu.edu/earth103/node/508

Refugee Camp in Mozambique. *Flickr.* https://www.flickr.com/photos/un_photo/4421127032

"Vapor". *Wikipedia.* https://en.wikipedia.org/wiki/Vapor

www.ingramcontent.com/pod-product-compliance
Lightning Source LLC
Chambersburg PA
CBHW060811090426
42737CB00002B/28